Creatures of the Deep

BLUNTNOSE SIXGILL SHARKS
AND OTHER STRANGE SHARKS

Rachel Lynette

Raintree

Chicago, Illinois

www.heinemannraintree.com
Visit our website to find out more information about Heinemann-Raintree books.

To order:

☎ Phone 888-454-2279

💻 Visit www.heinemannraintree.com to browse our catalog and order online.

©2012 Raintree
an imprint of Capstone Global Library, LLC
Chicago, Illinois

Edited by Megan Cotugno and Abby Colich
Designed by Philippa Jenkins
Illustrated by Terry Pastor / www. theartagency.co.uk
Picture research by Hannah Taylor
Originated by Capstone Global Library
Printed and bound in China by CTPS

15 14 13 12 11
10 9 8 7 6 5 4 3 2 1

Library of Congress Cataloging-in-Publication Data

Lynette, Rachel.
  Bluntnose sixgill sharks and other strange sharks / Rachel Lynette.—1st ed.
      p. cm.—(Creatures of the deep)
  Includes bibliographical references and index.
  ISBN 978-1-4109-4196-1 (hc)—ISBN 978-1-4109-4203-6 (pb) 1. Hexanchidae—Juvenile literature. 2. Sharks—Juvenile literature. I. Title.
  QL638.95.H48L96 2012
  597.3—dc22   2010038670

Acknowledgments
We would like to thank the following for permission to reproduce photographs:

© Veronica von Allwörden p. 16; Alamy Images p. 27 (© Amar and Isabelle Guillen - Guillen Photography); Corbis pp. 12 (© Stuart Westmorland), 22 (Science Faction/Norbert Wu); FLPA pp. 28 (Tui De Roy/Minden Pictures), 29 top (Norbert Wu/Minden Pictures); Getty Images p. 25 (AFP/TORU YAMANAKA); Image Quest Marine pp. 18, 19 (Kelvin Aitken); naturepl.com pp. 4, 6 (Brandon Cole), 24 (Bruce Rasner/Rotman); Photolibrary pp. 10 (OSF/Tobias Bernhard), 26 (Peter Arnold Images/Doug Perrine); SeaPics.com pp. 8, 11, 15, 17 (Eric H. Cheng), 20 (e-Photography/Hirose), 21 (David Shen), 23 (Michael S. Nolan); Shutterstock pp. 29 bottom (© Yize), 14 (© Michael Woodruff).

Cover photograph of Six Gill Shark (*Hexanchus griseus*) at Puget Sound, Seattle, Washington, reproduced with permission of Photolibrary (OSF/Howard Hall).

We would like to thank Michael Bright for his invaluable help in the preparation of this book.

CONTENTS

Some words are printed in bold, **like this.** You can find out what they mean by looking in the glossary.

GIANT OF THE DEEP

The bluntnose sixgill shark can reach lengths of more than 4.9 meters (16 feet)! If you and three friends lie down in a long line, your line would be about as long as a sixgill shark. It is the third largest meat-eating shark in the world.

A shark's torpedo-shaped body helps it to glide through the water.

What is a shark?

Sharks are a very old type of fish. Sharks have been swimming in the earth's oceans for more than 400 million years! Most sharks have grey, torpedo-shaped bodies. This body shape helps them swim quickly through the water. Sharks also have dorsal fins on their backs. The dorsal fin sticks straight up and keeps the shark from rolling over in the water.

No bones

Unlike most other fish, sharks do not have any bones. Instead they have **cartilage**. Cartilage is softer and lighter than bone. You have cartilage in your body, too. The tip of your nose is made from cartilage.

A bluntnose sixgill shark is nearly three times the size of a six-foot-tall man.

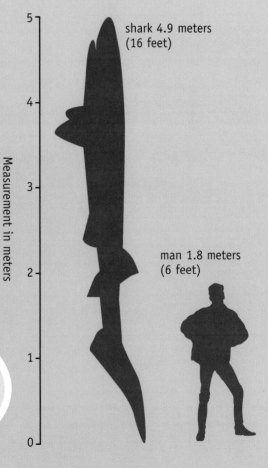

Measurement in meters

shark 4.9 meters (16 feet)

man 1.8 meters (6 feet)

AT HOME IN DEEP WATER

Bluntnose sixgill sharks can be found in oceans throughout the world, mostly in tropical and **temperate** waters. However, they have also been spotted as far north as Alaska and Iceland.

Staying below

During the day, bluntnose sixgill sharks spend their time in deep water. They may go down as deep as 1,830 meters (6,000 feet). That is more than a mile deep! At night they swim toward the surface to feed. Sixgill sharks are sensitive to light, so they cannot go near the surface during the daytime.

Sixgills live deep in the ocean because they are sensitive to light.

A Harsh Environment

It is very cold in deep water, and there is not much oxygen. There is also a lot of **pressure** from all of the water above. The deep ocean is very dark and there is not much to eat. Sixgill sharks are **adapted** to live in this harsh environment. Because people rarely go into deep waters, sixgills are usually observed at night when they swim up to shallow waters.

Bluntnose Sixgill Shark Locations

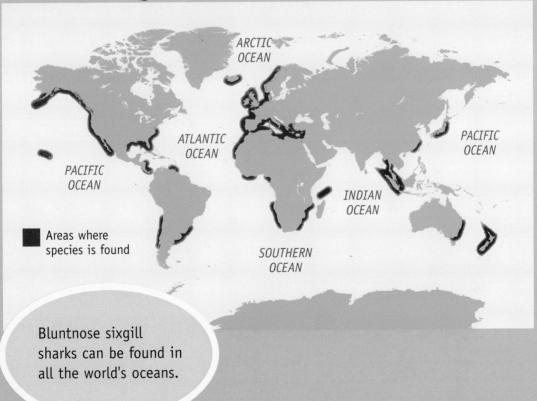

ARCTIC OCEAN

ATLANTIC OCEAN

PACIFIC OCEAN

PACIFIC OCEAN

INDIAN OCEAN

■ Areas where species is found

SOUTHERN OCEAN

Bluntnose sixgill sharks can be found in all the world's oceans.

SHARK PARTS

As its name suggests, the bluntnose sixgill shark has a blunt, rounded nose. It also has six **gill slits** on each side of its body. Most other sharks have only five. A sixgill shark has just one small dorsal fin, set close to the tail on its back. Sixgills have eyes that glow **fluorescent** green. A bluntnose sixgill shark's body can be grey, olive green, or brown. It is darker on top than on its underside. A sixgill shark also has a light stripe that runs across the side of its body.

The bluntnose sixgill shark's gills are just in front of its fin.

Two kinds of teeth

Bluntnose sixgill sharks have big mouths full of sharp teeth. They have different teeth on their top jaw than on their bottom jaw. On the top jaw, they have nine sharp teeth on each side. These teeth are long and slightly curved. On the bottom jaw, they have six saw-like teeth on each side.

This diagram shows the anatomy of a bluntnose sixgill shark.

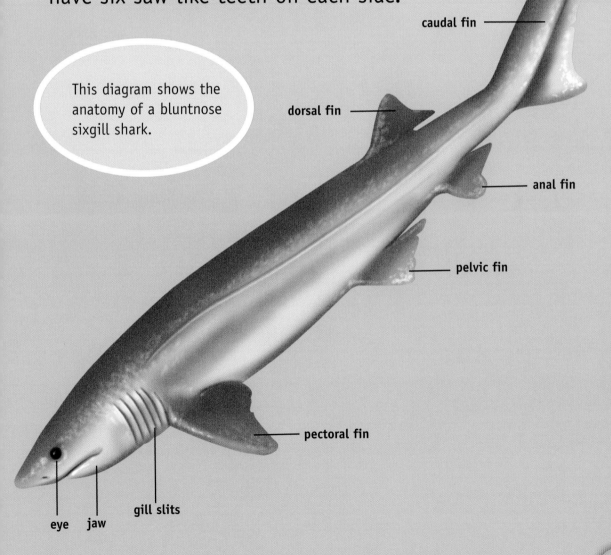

caudal fin

dorsal fin

anal fin

pelvic fin

pectoral fin

gill slits

eye jaw

TIME TO EAT

Bluntnose sixgill sharks hunt at night. They swim up toward the surface where there is more food. Sixgill sharks will eat just about anything they can find. Most of their diet consists of fish. They eat dolphins, flounders, cod, **rays**, and even other sharks. They also eat seals, shellfish, octopuses, and squid.

The octopus is common prey for the bluntnose sixgill shark.

Hunting prey

Sixgill sharks usually move slowly. But they can move in quick bursts when hunting. Sixgills swallow their food whole when they can. For bigger **prey**, they use their teeth to saw the flesh away from the bone. In addition to hunting, sixgills are also **scavengers** that will feast on the remains of dead animals.

In addition to killing prey, sixgills are also scavengers.

Boy Catches Shark

Sixgill sharks are most likely to encounter people when they are feeding in shallow water. In August 2009, nine-year-old Cosmo Miller caught a 68 kilogram (150 pound) sixgill shark near Seattle, Washington. After taking pictures, Cosmo released the shark back into the water and it swam away.

PLENTY OF PUPS

Scientists believe that sixgills **migrate** to shallow water to **breed** between May and November. The males court, or attract, the females by biting their fins.

This picture shows a pregnant sixgill shark.

Sixgill sharks are ovoviviparous. This means that the eggs hatch inside the mother. Scientists believe that sixgill sharks have a **gestation** period of about two years. The mother then gives birth to between 22 and 108 baby sixgills, which are called pups.

Life of a pup

Baby sixgills are about 60 centimeters (2 feet) long. They are lighter in color than adult sixgills. Their lighter color helps **camouflage** them in the shallow waters where they live until they reach adulthood. Despite their lighter color, many sixgill pups get eaten by bigger fish. Many of the fish that eat sixgill pups are the same **species** that the sixgills will later **prey** on, if they survive to adulthood. Sixgills grow slowly and live for about 80 years.

SIXGILLS IN SEATTLE

In Washington state, a place called Puget Sound has a large number of bluntnose sixgill sharks. Most of the sharks that have been observed there have been young. Researchers believe that Puget Sound may be a kind of nursery where young sharks live until they are ready to survive in deep water.

Puget Sound has a large population of bluntnose sixgill sharks.

Illegal in Washington

Fishing for sixgills has been illegal, or against the law, in Washington state since 2001. This may be one reason for the high number of sixgill sharks that are seen in Seattle.

Researching sharks

The Seattle Aquarium has built a research station on the seafloor just to study sixgills.

They use diving cages to stay safe while studying the sharks in their natural environment. They also use underwater video cameras. Researchers watch six video monitors to observe the sixgills. They are usually between 1.8 and 2.1 meters (6 to 7 feet), but can grow as large as 4.9 meters (16 feet).

This cage keeps researchers safe while they observe sixgill sharks.

STUDYING SIXGILLS

One way for **marine biologists** to learn about bluntnose sixgill sharks is to **tag** them. Once a sixgill is tagged, it can be identified and its behavior can be studied.

Researchers at the Seattle Aquarium attach 30-centimeter (12-inch) bright yellow tags to sixgills as they swim by the underwater dive cage. Each tag has a different set of up to four symbols. When divers see a sixgill with a tag, they can identify the sixgill by the symbols on the tag. Then they can report information, such as their size and location, back to the aquarium.

This sixgill can be identified by the symbols on its tag.

These young sixgills will travel together for a few years.

All in the Family

Researchers also take a small sample of flesh from the sixgill that they use for genetic testing. The genetic testing tells the researchers whether or not different sixgills are related to each other. By tagging sixgills, biologists have discovered that young sixgills from the same **litter** often travel together for the first few years of their lives.

FRILLED SHARK

Frilled sharks look like **mythical** sea monsters! They are about 1.8 meters (6 feet) long with slender, eel-shaped bodies and lizard-like heads. The frilled shark gets its name from its six-frilled **gill slits**.

Mouths and teeth

Frilled sharks have huge mouths. They have 300 teeth that are arranged in 25 rows around the jaw. Each tooth is a bit like a mini pitchfork with three sharp points. Scientists think that squid, which make up a good portion of the frilled shark's diet, get caught in the teeth when the shark opens its huge mouth. Frilled sharks also eat other fish, both large and small.

A frilled shark is about as long as a full-grown human.

Frilled sharks have huge mouths with 300 teeth.

Living fossils

Frilled sharks have been called living fossils because they have changed very little from their prehistoric ancestors. Frilled sharks are rarely seen by humans because they live in very deep water. At times in history, it was thought the shark was **extinct** because one had not been seen in so long.

GOBLIN SHARK

Goblin sharks are frightening creatures! They are about 3.7 meters (12 feet) long and have soft, pink bodies. They have large, flat blade-like snouts. Under their snouts, goblin sharks have large mouths with long, inward curving teeth.

A goblin shark is twice as long as an adult human.

A goblin shark can open its mouth very wide and **protrude** its jaws.

Sensing Prey

Goblin sharks feed on fish, shrimp, squid, octopus, and crabs. A goblin shark finds its **prey** in the dark depths of the ocean with special electro-sensitive organs called *ampullae of Lorenzini* that are in its snout. To catch prey, the goblin shark opens its mouth very quickly and very wide. It then uses a tongue-like organ to suck the prey into its sharp front teeth.

A Goblin Shark Mystery

Goblin sharks are rarely seen by humans. However, in 2003 more than 100 goblin sharks were caught off the coast of Taiwan—in a place they had never been seen before. Scientists believe that the presence of so many goblin sharks might be the result of an earthquake that had just occurred in the area.

COOKIECUTTER SHARK

The cookiecutter shark is small at just 51 centimeters (20 inches) long. It has a torpedo-shaped body. The underside of the shark is covered with small light-producing organs called photophores. The photophores make a green glow to attract **prey**. The cookiecutter shark has remarkable teeth. They are large and triangle-shaped on the bottom jaw, and smaller but still sharp on the top jaw.

The cookiecutter shark uses its lips to form a suction on its prey.

One bite at a time

The cookiecutter shark is known for taking single, crater-shaped bites from much larger animals such as marlins, tuna, whales, and seals. It does this by sealing its lips onto the larger animal to make a suction. Then it digs its lower teeth into the prey's flesh and spins its body around to remove a circular plug of flesh from the prey. Many different animals have been found with the perfectly round wounds of cookiecutter sharks.

This dolphin has been bitten by a cookiecutter shark.

MEGAMOUTH SHARK

The megamouth is a rarely seen, large, sluggish shark that can reach lengths of up to 5.5 meters (18 feet) long. Its body is soft and flabby with loose skin. The megamouth is named for its huge mouth that is full of many tiny teeth.

The megamouth shark has many small teeth.

An Amazing Discovery

The very first megamouth shark to be seen and documented by humans was in 1976. That was when one was accidentally caught by a U.S. Navy ship off the coast of Hawaii. A second one was not caught until 1984. There have only been 49 confirmed sightings of the megamouth shark.

Eating habits

Even though it is a large shark with a large mouth, the megamouth is not a threat to most fish and other sea life. This is because the megamouth is a filter feeder. It eats only very small animals such as **krill**, small fish, and **plankton**. The megamouth eats by opening its large mouth and sucking its **prey** inside.

Megamouth sharks are filter feeders.

TOP OF THE FOOD CHAIN

Most sharks are fierce **predators**. Often, they are at the top of the food chain and have few, if any, natural predators. Sharks are an important link in the food chain because they help to limit the number of other animals by eating them.

Sharks are fierce predators.

Sharks eat animals that prey on shellfish like these.

Food chain

If sharks were removed from the food chain, other **species** might overpopulate the ocean. When there are too many of a particular species, that species is in danger of running out of food. Other species that eat the same food may also be in danger. That can happen more easily in deep water where there is less food than in other parts of the ocean. In a food chain, a change in just one species affects many other animals.

Good-bye Sharks, Good-bye Shellfish

In some communities where people have killed a lot of sharks, they have also lost most of their shellfish. That happened because the sharks were not there to eat the fish that eat the shellfish. This caused more shellfish to be eaten.

SAVE OUR SHARKS

Although some **species** of shark may be **endangered**, they are rarely protected by law. Sharks are often fished for sport, meat, or fins. They are also caught accidently in the large nets of commercial fishermen. Sharks that are caught by accident are rarely returned to the ocean alive. About 100 million sharks are killed by people each year. **Environmentalists** are concerned that some rare species of shark could become **extinct**.

People kill about 100 million sharks every year.

Don't Eat that Soup!

In China there is a high demand for shark fin soup, which is usually served for special occasions. Because people only want the fins and not the rest of the shark, many fishermen cut the fins off the shark while it is still alive. Then they return the shark to the sea. The shark cannot swim without fins, so it sinks to the bottom and dies a slow death.

Many sharks are killed just so their fins can be used to make soup.

GLOSSARY

adapt to change to adjust to conditions in the environment

breed to mate

camouflage coloring or marks that help an animal blend in with its environment

cartilage hard but flexible material that forms a shark's skeleton

endangered at risk or in danger

environmentalist person who works to protect nature

extinct died out completely

fluorescent very bright color

gestation time that it takes a baby to grow inside the mother

gill slit slit in a shark or other fish's body that is used for breathing

krill very small shrimp-like animals with hard shells

litter group of babies born at the same time from the same mother

marine biologist scientist who studies plants and animals in the ocean

migrate to move from one place to another

mythical word used to describe imaginary place or creature found in stories

plankton simple plant-like organisms that live in the water

predator animal that hunts another animal for food

pressure force pressed on something

prey animal that is hunted by another animal; to hunt another animal

protrude to jut out of something

ray wide, flat fish

scavenger animal that feeds on dead plant and animal material and waste

species type of plant or animal

tag use of a marker to identify an animal

temperate area that is neither very hot nor very cold

FIND OUT MORE

Books

Hajeski, Nancy. *Sharks (Hammond Undercover)*. Duncan, S.C.: Hammond, 2010.

Wagner, Obe. *The Everything Kids' Sharks Book*. Avon, Mass.: Adams Media, 2005.

Wilsdon, Christina. *Sharks*, Pleasantville, N.Y.: Gareth Stevens, 2009.

Websites

http://dsc.discovery.com/videos/shark-week-six-gill-shark.html
Visit this site to watch a Discovery Channel video on the sixgill shark.

www.seasky.org/deep-sea/sixgill-shark.html
Learn about creatures of the deep, including the sixgill shark.

www.seattleaquarium.org/NetCommunity/Page.aspx?pid=456&srcid=271
Discover more about the Seattle Aquarium's research on sixgill sharks.

INDEX